TAYLOR SWIFT A BIOGRAPHY

The great story of a famous pop star icon, Taylor swift, her modest beginning from being a small town country single to the most well-known and popular musicians of our time

Written by:

Toby Lowe

Contents

Chapter One: Early Age

On December 13, 1989, Taylor Alison Swift was born in Reading, Pennsylvania. Swift grew up working on the Christmas tree farm owned by her family in rural Wyomissing. Swift quickly followed in the musical footsteps of her opera-singing grandma. By the age of ten, Swift was performing at a range of neighborhood activities, such as fairs and competitions. At age 11, she performed "The Star-Spangled Banner" at a Philadelphia 76ers basketball game. At age 12, she started writing her own songs and picking up the guitar.

Swift frequently traveled to Nashville, Tennessee, the center of country music, to further her musical career. She co-wrote songs there and sought to get a recording deal there. Swift's family relocated to nearby Hendersonville, Tennessee, in an effort to advance her profession when people noticed her commitment.

The Alvernia Montessori School served as her preschool and elementary school. Taylor and his younger brother were brought up as Presbyterians and spent every summer vacation attending Bible school. She started attending Wyomissing Junior/Senior High School and the West Reading Elementary Center after she and her family relocated to Wyomissing (Pennsylvania).

She developed an interest in musical theater at the age of nine and started acting in Berks Youth Theater Academy shows. She typically took singing and acting lessons on Broadway.

Taylor was influenced by country music as she performed at local fairs, festivals, cafes, and karaoke events.

She wrote the songs for the album during her freshman year of high school, focusing on love themes with country music styles and pop. The first studio album, "Taylor

Swift," was released on October 24, 2006, under the record company Big Machine Records. Her offspring's singles were included on the most significant lists.

At the Academy of Country Music Awards (ACM) on May 15, 2007, she performed "Tim McGraw."

Her second single, "Teardrops on My Guitar," was released on February 24 and peaked at number two on the country charts and number 33 on the Billboard Hot 100.

She received the Nashville Composers Association Award for best vocalist and songwriter in the month of October. In addition, she created a Christmas EP titled "Sounds of the Season" that she launched for sale on October 16 and that was only offered at Target Corporation, helping it to match the success of her debut album.

The third single, "Our Song," which was released on November 7, 2007, spent six weeks at the top of the country charts.

On September 12, 2008, she made her debut with her most popular track, "Love Story." This song was the first of its kind in country music. Romeo and Juliet served as inspiration for the song's music video.

She wrote all the songs on her second studio album, "Fearless," which was released in the US on November 11. It debuted at number one on the Billboard 200, was the country music album with the highest sales, and was the fourth best seller that year. It was one of the biggest sellers in that nation, and this album was presented at Madison Square Garden.

Fearless' "White Horse" (the album's second single) made its debut on December 8th, 2008.

Taylor became the youngest artist to win the "Album of the Year" award at the 44th Academy of Country Music Awards when she got it for her album Fearless.

Taylor Swift talked about her debut tour, which included stops in fifty-two locations across thirty-eight provinces and states, in January 2009. There was a six-month break in both the US and Canada. On April 23, the tour kicked off in Evansville, Indiana.

For her single "Love Story," which is the most decorated country album in history, she received best female video of the year and video of the year at the CMT Music Awards in June.

Taylor debuted in the movie Valentine's Day at the beginning of 2010 in a supporting role for the soundtrack's official song, "Today Was a Fairytale."

She told her followers online on July 20 that her third album, "Speak Now," would be released on October 25. She wrote all 14 songs on that album, with "Mine" serving as the lead single.

The first dates of the tour were announced in September 2010, and it began in February 2011 and would visit 18 different nations before wrapping up in 2012.

She received a nomination for "Best Female Video of the Year" at the 2010 MTV Video Music Awards on September 12, 2010, which took place amidst controversy over the 2009 ceremony.

On March 19, 2011, she gave a performance at the Sports Palace of the Community of Madrid during her maiden trip to Spain.

The first single, "We Are Never Ever Getting Back Together," was released on August 13 and became Taylor Swift's first number one on the Billboard Hot 100. Her new album, "Red," was released on October 22, 2012.

She debuted her track "Ronan" on September 7 at the Stand Up To Cancer gala; the song was written in honor of a four-year-old kid who passed away from cancer. She contributed the songs Safe & Sound and Eyes Open to the soundtrack of The Hunger Games that same year.

It was presented at the Kids' Choice Awards 2012 with the award "The Big Help" (The Big Help), given by Michelle Obama in recognition of her efforts to aid the less fortunate around the globe, including those impacted by tornadoes in the United States and those affected by the rains in Colombia, among others; and with his project "Speak Now, Help Now." She launched the Red Tour in 45 different cities on March 13, 2013. She started writing the tracks for her fifth studio album in the month of July.

Taylor revealed the details of her upcoming fifth studio album on August 18, 2014, during a live event that was carried on Yahoo. Her latest album, "1989," a Pop record with 80s influences, was released on October 27, 2014. Swift produced two singles: "Shake It Off," which peaked at No. 1 on the Billboard Hot 100 on August 27, and "Blank Space," which featured this theme and seized the top spot for the first time ever.

The singer received the Video of the Year award with Bad Blood on August 30, 2015, along with the best pop video with Blank Space and the best female video at the MTV Awards. Taylor Swift debuted the music video for Look What You Made Me in August 2017, the lead single from her upcoming album "Reputation," which will be out on November 10.

Chapter two: Education and Honors

The 32-year-old is now a member of the class of 2022 after receiving an honorary doctorate in fine arts from New York University. Taylor Swift, or Dr. Swift as she is now known, was also awarded the privilege of delivering the commencement address at the event on May 18 at Yankee Stadium.

Taylor Swift shared a reel on her Instagram and TikTok that clearly demonstrated how excited she was for the commencement. Her reference to the fact that she would be wearing a cap and gown for the first time in the caption served to emphasize this point.

The pop artist said in her commencement speech that she had never gone to college because of the chaos of launching her career at the tender age of 15. However, she added that as a child, she had always hoped for a "normal college experience"

"I never had the typical college experience in the traditional sense. Up to the tenth grade, I attended a public high school, then I completed my education by working on home-school assignments on the floors of airline terminals. Growing up, I always saw myself attending college and seeing the posters I would place in my freshman dorm.

Taylor Swift attended Hendersonville High School in Hendersonville, Tennessee, where she began her high school career, but she switched to Aaron Academy after her sophomore year. Because of the latter, she was able to balance her education and burgeoning profession by being home-schooled. Swift, who is never one to get bogged down, graduated a year early and with a flawless 4.0 GPA.

She added it to her bucket list, but the desire to "get a college degree... somehow, someway" persisted. Taylor Swift hasn't been able to complete her education the conventional way, but thanks to this honorary doctorate, her wish may have been partially realized.

Taylor Swift's commencement address was as smart and humorous as it was moving and inspirational. The singer thanked NYU for making her "technically, on paper at least, a doctor," making light of the fact that she wouldn't be the kind of doctor people would want on hand in an emergency unless it involved identifying an excessive amount of cat species or composing great songs.

Swift gave what she called "life hacks" rather than general, unwanted advise, saying:

Life can be difficult, particularly if you try to carry everything at once. Catch and release is a component of maturing and entering new life chapters. Knowing what to hold onto and what to let go is what I mean by that. Select what you want to keep and let the rest go. What your life has time and space for is entirely up to you. Keep an open mind.

In addition, Taylor Swift taught a very important lesson about overcoming the stigma associated with being eager and prepared to work hard:

"I strongly believe in expressing your excitement for things. In our society of "unbothered ambivalence," excitement seems to be stigmatized in a misleading way. Never feel guilty about trying. Inefficiency is a myth.

Swift told the grads the hard fact that those who strive for excellence like themselves will undoubtedly "screw it up sometimes," but he then gave them the solace that this doesn't mean they failed. She uttered:

"You'll make mistakes occasionally. I will also. We'll bounce back. It will teach us something. Because of that, we will become more resilient. We will breathe in; breathe out, through, and deeply as long as we are lucky enough to be breathing. I am a doctor now, therefore I am aware of how breathing functions.

The singer-songwriter invited the graduating class to "keep dancing like we're the Class of '22" as a fitting tribute to the song's lyrics.

CHAPTER THREE: Country Music Career

A stellar performance at The Bluebird Café in Nashville helped Swift get a contract with Scott Borchetta's Big Machine Records. She released her first single, "Tim McGraw," in 2006, and the song became a Top 10 hit on the country charts. It also appeared on her self-titled debut album in October of that same year, which went on to sell more than 5 million copies. More popular singles soon followed, including "Our Song," a No. 1 country music hit. "Teardrops on My Guitar," "Picture to Burn" and "Should've Said No" were also successful tracks.

Swift also received critical praise for her debut effort. She won the Horizon Award from the Country Music Association (CMA) and the Academy of Country Music (ACM) Award for Top New Female Vocalist in 2007. Swift next released Sounds of the Season: The Taylor Swift Holiday Collection that year. Her renditions of "Silent Night" and "Santa Baby" were modest hits on the country charts.

Every Tuesday after school in Nashville, Taylor began creating songs with songwriter Liz Rose for two hours. She later became the Sony/ATV publishing house's youngest performer signed, however she departed the band at age 14. Because she wanted to document the early years of her life on an album while they still accurately reflected the struggles she was through, she thought she was running out of time.

Swift attracted Scott Borchetta's eye at a showcase at Nashville's Bluebird Cafe in 2005. At the time, Borchetta was getting ready to launch Big Machine Records, an indie record label. Her father bought a 3% stake in Big Machine, making her one of the company's initial signees.

Taylor then began work on her debut album and convinced Big Machine to work with Nathan Chapman as her song producer. The self-titled album by Taylor Swift was released on October 24, 2006, following the release of her first lead single, "Tim McGraw," in June 2006. On the US Billboard 200, where it spent 275 weeks, it peaked at number 5. Swift spent 2006 and 2007 promoting her album on radios, television, and as the opening act for country musicians in the US. Swift was also the opening act for Brad Paisley's 2007 tour. Taylor released four additional singles from her debut album in 2007 and 2008, and each of them debuted on the Hot Country Songs chart of Billboard.

Swift's first two EPs, "The Taylor Swift Holiday Collection" and "Beautiful Eyes," were released in October 2007 and July 2008, respectively. All three of her debut albums received positive reviews.

At the 50th Grammy Awards, she broke the record for being the youngest person to win Best New Artist.

CHAPTER FOUR: Taylor swifts' albums

Fearless

Fearless, Swift's second album, was released on November 11th, 2008. Throughout 2008 and 2009, five songs were released, with the first single, "Love Story," reaching its peak at number four on the Billboard Hot 100 list and number one in Australia. In the US, "You Belong With Me" reached its highest point at number two. The album was the best-selling one in the US in 2009 and debuted at the top of the Billboard 200.

Swift's first headlining concert tour, The Fearless Tour, brought in over $63 million, and Taylor published a documentary about the tour that was shown on television and made available on DVD. With this album, Swift received several prizes in 2009 and 2010 at illustrious award ceremonies like the CMAs and the ACMs. She also won Artist of the Year at the AMAs and her first Album of the Year trophy at the 52nd Grammy accolades, where she also took home three more accolades. Billboard also recognized her as "Female Artist of the Year" in 2009.

Taylor also co-wrote songs with musicians including John Mayer, Boys including Girls, and Kellie Pickler. She also composed the songs "Crazier" and "You'll Always Find Your Way Back Home" for the Hannah Montana album on the Disney Channel.

Taylor also contributed "Today Was A Fairytale" to the Valentine's Day soundtrack during the Fearless period; the song reached its US peak at number two.

Speak Now

"Mine," the first single from Swift's third studio album, Speak Now, was released in

August 2010. On the US Billboard Hot 100 list, it debuted at position three. Swift wrote every one of the 17 songs for her third album alone, and she also co-produced each song, in response to criticism that said Taylor's songwriting was strong because she collaborated with other authors.

On October 25, 2010, the album was released, debuting at the top of the Billboard 200 with one million copies sold in its first week.

Swift won Best Country Song and Best Country Solo Performance for "Mean" at the 54th Grammy Awards in 2012. She sang the song at the event as a reaction to her much criticized 2010 Grammy performance and to showcase her musical prowess.

Swift received several honors with Speak Now, including the BMI Award for Songwriter of the Year, the ACM and CMA Award for Entertainer of the Year, and the Billboard Woman of the Year title. Critics generally praised the album, with Rolling Stone hailing Taylor's prowess as a rockstar.

Between 2011 and 2012, the Speak Now World Tour was conducted, bringing in approximately $123 million. The "Speak Now World Tour Live" live CD was published in November 2011 by the performer.

Swift also provided two original songs, "Eyes Open" and "Safe & Sound," which were both recorded with The Civil Wars, to the soundtrack for The Hunger Games. The latter went on to get a Grammy nomination and a Golden Globe award. Taylor contributed to the May 2012 song "Both of Us" by BoB.

Red

The first single from Swift's fourth studio album, RED, "We Are Never Ever Getting Back Together," was made available in August 2012. Only 50 minutes after its release, it topped the iTunes digital song sales list, becoming her first number one in the US and New Zealand. Her third song, "I Knew You Were Trouble," climbed at number two on the Billboard Hot 100 and in the top five of the world's most significant music market nations.

Release day for RED was October 22, 2012. For this album, Taylor collaborated with composers and producers that would later become important to her career, including Max Martin and Shellback, as well as longtime collaborators Nathan Chapman and Liz Rose. Heartland rock, dubstep, and dance pop influences are among the new genres that Swift has included throughout the album.

Swift's first number-one album in the UK was RED, which also debuted at number one in the US with 1.2 million copies sold in its first week. The Red Tour, which took place between March 2013 and June 2014 and brought in more than $150 million, was the highest-earning national tour at its conclusion.

Swift received several honors for Red, including four Grammy nominations, a VMA trophy, many AMA statues, and a BMI Songwriter of the Year award. The Country Music Academy also presented Taylor with a Pinnacle Award.

Taylor recorded "Sweeter than Fiction" in 2013 for the soundtrack of the film One Chance. It was her debut endeavor with producer Jack Antonoff, with whom she would later collaborate again. Taylor also worked on "Highway Don't Care," one of the most popular country songs of that year, alongside Tim McGraw and Keith Urban.

1989

Taylor relocated to New York City in March 2014 to begin work on 1989, her fifth studio album, which would go on to become her most popular and longest-charting album. Swift broke away from the rural vibe of her earlier albums and positioned 1989 as her "first documented, official pop album" while drawing inspiration from 1980s synth-pop. On October 27, 2014, the album was published, and in its first week, 1.28 million copies were sold in the US, debuting at the top of the Billboard 200 list.

Three of its songs, including "Shake It Off," "Blank Space," and "Bad Blood," which features rapper Kendrick Lamar, peaked at number one in the US, Australia, and Canada.

The highest-grossing tour of the year, with $250 million in total sales, was the 1989 World Tour, which took place from May through December 2015.

Taylor fought against two of the largest streaming services in the world at the time, Apple Music and Spotify, in an attempt to disapprove of the way these businesses compensated musicians. Swift deleted her entire discography off Spotify in November 2014, claiming that the free, ad-supported version of the site undercut the paid, premium service, which pays greater royalties to composers. Taylor criticized Apple Music in an open letter he published in June 2015 for not paying musicians royalties during the three-month free trial period of the streaming service. Apple said the next day that it will compensate artists throughout the free trial period.

Swift earned the first-ever Dick Clark Award for Excellence at the 2014 American Music Awards after being voted Billboard's Woman of the Year in 2014. Swift also won a BRIT, many VMAs, and numerous other awards during this time period, making 1989 the most decorated pop decade ever.

1989 won three categories at the 58th Grammy Awards in 2016, including Album of the Year. As a main artist, Swift became the sixth act overall and the first female to win Album of the Year twice.

Swift co-wrote "This Is What You Came For" with Calvin Harris in 2016 and "I Don't Wanna Live Forever" for the Fifty Shades Darker soundtrack with Zayn Malik at the beginning of 2017. The song was awarded Best Collaboration at the 2017 MTV Video Music Awards and peaked at number two in the US.

Taylor wrote "Better Man" during the Red period, and it was included on Little Big Town's seventh album, The Breaker. Swift won Song of the Year at the 51st CMA Awards in 2017 for this song.

Reputation

With her sixth studio album, reputation, Swift had one of the most successful comebacks in history after spending the most of 2016 largely avoiding social media and the general public. The first track from the album, "Look What You Made Me Do," broke the record for most views in the first 24 hours after release.

The album, which had a strong electro pop style with hip hop, R&B, and EDM elements, was released on November 10, 2017. With 1.21 million copies sold in its first week, it debuted at the top of the Billboard 200. With this accomplishment, Swift made history by being the first performer to sell one million copies of four albums in the US in a single week. Three further foreign singles were produced by the project, including the US top-five hit "...Ready for It?"

She started her reputation Stadium Tour in promotion of reputation, which lasted from May to November 2018. The tour broke Swift's own record for the highest-grossing US tour by a woman, which was previously held by her 1989 World Tour ($181.5 million), with box office receipts of $266.1 million and over two million tickets sold. Additionally, it became as the most successful North American concert tour in history. The tour brought in $345.7 million globally. Swift's reputation Stadium Tour concert footage was made available on Netflix on December 31.

At the 2019 Grammy Awards, Reputation was nominated for Best Pop Vocal Album. Swift received four honors at the 2018 AMAs, including the Artist of the Year and Favorite Pop/Rock Female Artist trophies. Swift won a total of 23 trophies during the 2018 event, becoming her the most-awarded female singer in AMA history.

Lover

Following the signing of a new multi-album contract with Universal Music Group in November 2018, Taylor's next albums will be marketed under the Republic Records banner. She was given permission to keep ownership of her master recordings as part of the deal. Swift would own her first studio album, her eighth, when it was released.

Swift became the first female artist to accomplish this feat when her album Lover, which was released on August 23, 2019, became Taylor's sixth straight album to sell over 500,000 copies in its first week in the US. Setting a record for the most concurrent entries by a woman, all 18 of the album's tracks made it into the Billboard Hot 100 list in the same week. 2019's best-selling solo studio album globally, Lover, sold 3.2 million units.

The album received several honors, including 3 Grammy nominations, 3 VMA nominations, and 6 AMA nominations. Swift also made history by being the first female musician to take home the American Music Award for musician of the Decade.

In the Cats movie version of Andrew Lloyd Webber's musical, Taylor played Bombalurina. She co-wrote and recorded the original song "Beautiful Ghosts" for the film, which resulted to her receiving a Grammy nomination and another Golden Globe nomination at the 63rd Annual GRAMMY Awards.

A portion of her life and career are covered in the documentary "Miss Americana," which had its world debut at the 2020 Sundance Film Festival and was made available on Netflix in January of the same year. The original song "Only the Young" from Miss Americana was written by Swift after the 2018 US presidential elections.

Swift got involved in a well-publicized dispute with manager Scooter Braun and her previous label Big Machine over the ownership of the rights of her back catalog while promoting her album Lover in 2019. She said that despite her repeated attempts, Big Machine would only enable her to purchase the masters if she agreed to trade a new record for an older one under a different contract, which she refused to sign. Swift's masters, videos, and artwork were reportedly sold to Shamrock Holdings for $300 million in October 2019. In an attempt to take ownership of and control over her music and life's work, Swift started re-

Recording her back catalog in November 2020.

Folklore, evermore and re-recordings

Swift unexpectedly revealed on July 23, 2020, that she will be releasing folklore, her eighth studio album, at midnight. With 8 non-consecutive weeks at the top of the chart, the album became the year's longest-running #1 after debuting at #1 on the Billboard 200. "Carigan," the album's main song, likewise debuted at the top spot.

Folklore was created independently during the COVID-19 epidemic in cooperation with Taylor's longtime musical collaborator Jack Antonoff, Aaron Dessner of The National, with whom Taylor had never previously collaborated, and Bon Iver, who are featured on one of the album's songs.

Swift self-directed "folklore: the long pond studio sessions" was made available on Disney+ in November 2020. In the documentary, Taylor, Aaron, and Jack play all of the songs on the album while explaining the meanings and inspirations behind it.

Swift received 5 Grammy nominations for Folklore, including Album and Song of the Year. Taylor became the first woman to get the Grammy's top award three times as she took home the Album of the Year trophy.

Swift stunned her fans one again on December 10, 2020, when she revealed the title of her ninth studio album and folklore's sibling record, evermore. Taylor's work with Bon Iver, Aaron Dessner, Jack Antonoff, and others were maintained on the 11th album, which also welcomed new musicians into the "folkmore universe" including HAIM and The National. Evermore and its lead song "willow" both entered at the top of the Billboard 200 and Hot 100 charts. Swift became the first artist to twice debut at the top of the singles and albums charts by having both sister albums accomplish this feat.

Swift's earlier cheery pop albums have been replaced by an indie folk and alternative rock production on Folklore and Evermore. Both albums sold over a million copies globally in their first week, and Folklore set a new mark for the number of female artists' first-day Spotify album streams.

In November of last year, Taylor started working on the re-recordings of her first six studio albums. Fearless (Taylor's Version), a re-recording of her second album Fearless, was the first product of this initiative to acquire her back catalog. In addition to the 20 tracks that had already been published in 2008 and 2009, it also had six previously unheard songs that were not initially included in the album. It was released on April 9, 2021. Swift's ninth consecutive album, Fearless (Taylor's Version), debuted at #1 on the Billboard Hot 200, becoming the first re-recorded album in history to do so.

On November 19, 2021, Taylor will release the re-recorded version of her fourth studio album, RED.

Midnights'

Swift released her 10th studio album 'Midnights' at midnight on October 21, 2022. Three hours later, she released seven extra tracks in a deluxe version titled 'Midnights (3 am Edition).' The album broke new ground for the already prolific Swift, making her the first artist to have a song on all of the top 10 slots on the Billboard Hot 100 chart.

CHAPTER FIVE: Personal Life

Swift's alleged relationship with Joe Jonas of the well-known musical group The Jonas Brothers was the subject of rumors for the whole of 2008. Swift and Jonas did not recognize their connection. Swift claimed during the 2008 MTV Video Music Awards that anybody would be blessed to be dating him because "he's an amazing guy." Whatever the case, by the time Fearless was published, their relationship had apparently soured. The song, "Forever & Always," is allegedly about Jonas.

Swift and Taylor Lautner, an actor and one of the main characters in the popular Twilight franchise, were then romantically related. The two are said to have met while shooting Swift's big-screen debut, Valentine's Day, which was released in 2010. Sadly, the pair didn't last long enough to attend the premiere together since they split up in late 2009. Swift and Mayer then had a short relationship that ended amicably when Swift penned the exposé song "Dear John" about the womanizer.

From there, between 2010 and 2012, Swift was romantically connected to Jake Gyllenhaal and Glee actor Cory Monteith, as well as to Conor Kennedy, the son of Robert F. Kennedy Jr. She spent the last few months of 2012 dating another famous person, spending the first few days of 2013 with Harry Styles of One Direction. Swift dated musician, DJ, and music producer Calvin Harris in 2015; however, the pair allegedly split in June 2016. Actor Tom Hiddleston and Swift started dating shortly after, but the relationship ended three months later.

Joe Alwyn, an actor, and Swift have been dating since October 2016. The actor served as the inspiration for songs like "Gorgeous" and "Call It What You Want" on her reputation album. The duo met at the 2016 Met Gala.

Feud with Katy Perry

Katy Perry and Swift, who both dated John Mayer, broke up after Perry reportedly attempted to snatch several of Swift's stage dancers. Her conflict with Perry served as the inspiration for "Bad Blood." Swift said to Rolling Stone in 2014 that she "was never sure for years if we were friends or not." "At award shows, she would approach me, say something, and leave, and I would wonder if we were friends or if she had just uttered the harshest insult of my life?"

Then, in Swift's opinion, Perry went too far. Swift says, "She did something so horrible." 'Oh, we're simply straight out adversaries,' I thought. Not even about a boy, either! It was related to business. She essentially attempted to ruin a full stadium tour. She attempted to recruit a lot of people to get rid of me. Additionally, I'm remarkably non-confrontational considering how much I detest confrontations. I now have to stay away from her. I find it uncomfortable and dislike it.

Swift received a genuine olive branch from Perry on May 8, 2018, along with a message that said, "I've been doing some reflecting on past miscommunication and hurt feelings between us." This put an end to their conflict.

Scooter Braun and Album Ownership

Swift expressed her disappointment in June 2019 when she learned that her previous label had sold the library of her songs from her first six albums, up to reputation, to a business run by Scooter Braun, the manager of artists like Justin Bieber and Ariana Grande, whom she accused of using bullying techniques. She said on Tumblr that "Scooter has stripped me of my life's work,

that I wasn't given an opportunity to buy."
In essence, the fate of my artistic legacy will
soon be in the hands of those who sought to
destroy it. Swift said she will re-record her
older songs to reclaim creative and financial
control of her library just before the August
23 release of Lover.

In October 2020, Swift's catalog was once
again sold to Shamrock Holdings for around
$300 million. "As you are aware, I have
been aggressively attempting to reclaim
custody of my master recordings for the last
year. My team sought to negotiate with
Scooter Braun with that objective in mind,"
Swift stated on Twitter. "Before we even
looked at the financial records of BMLG
(which is usually the first step in an
acquisition of this sort), Scooter's team
wanted me to sign an unbreakable NDA
declaring I would never utter another thing
about Scooter Braun unless it was good.
Therefore, before I had the opportunity to

submit a bid for my own job, I would have to sign a paper that would permanently silence me. My legal team said that this is CERTAINLY NOT typical and that they have never seen an NDA handled in this manner unless it was to buy off an accusation of assault. He never even offered to provide my team a pricing quotation. These master recordings weren't offered to me for purchase. Swift proceeded by saying that she is now re-recording some of her earlier songs.

Swift said that she would release "Love Story," the first song from her next album, at midnight on February 11, 2021. Swift said the whole re-recorded album would be released later in 2021, and the song is from her Fearless album.

Sexual Assault Trial and Copyright Lawsuit

After 1989's enormous success, Swift took a vacation from the limelight. But in August 2017, she made a comeback when she testified in a case against David Mueller, a former radio DJ she had accused of molesting her in 2013. Swift's claims were refuted by Mueller, who claimed the event lost him his job. As a result, in 2015, he filed a lawsuit against Swift, her mother, and a radio station employee. In 2017, a jury found in Swift's favor when she countersued him for claimed assault and violence, giving her $1 in symbolic damages.

"I acknowledge the privilege that I benefit from in life, in society, and in my ability to shoulder the enormous cost of defending myself in a trial like this," Swift said in a statement after the judgment. Helping people whose voices ought to be heard is my hope. I will thus soon donate to a number of groups that support sexual assault victims in their efforts to defend themselves.

In the same year, Swift also found herself the target of a lawsuit from two composers who claimed she plagiarized their lyric from "Playas Gon' Play" for her popular song "Shake It Off." Even though a judge rejected the lawsuit in the beginning of 2018, stating that the "allegedly infringed lyrics are short phrases that lack the modicum of originality and creativity required for copyright protection," an appeals court reopened the case in October 2019.

Cats' and 'Miss Americana'

Swift appeared in a live-action version of the well-known Broadway musical Cats in December 2019, together with Jennifer Hudson, James Corden, and

Rebel Wilson. The song "Beautiful Ghosts," which she co-wrote with Andrew Lloyd Webber, is from the musical Cats.

The top-charting artist later received solo credit for the film Miss Americana, which documented the recording of her most recent studio albums as well as other well-known occasions including her sexual assault conviction. Before receiving a restricted theatrical release and being made available on Netflix, Miss Americana had its world debut at the Sundance Film Festival in January 2020.

2009 VMAs and Kanye West

At the 2009 CMT Music Awards, "Love Story" won Video of the Year and Female

Video of the Year for Swift, who also won numerous other prizes for her work on Fearless. Swift became the first country music artist to win a VMA in the same year when she won Best Female Video at the MTV Video Music Awards for her performance of "You Belong With Me." Rapper Kanye West's assertion that R&B singer Beyoncé should have received Swift's prize during her acceptance speech during the controversy-sparked triumph.

West was booted from the ceremony after Swift, who was visibly shocked, was unable to deliver her victory speech. Swift's speech was interrupted by Beyoncé, who later in the program brought her to the stage to receive her award for Best Video of the Year. Later, West expressed his regret to Swift in private and publicly on The Jay Leno Show.

Philanthropic Efforts and More Accolades

Swift, who earned $57 million in 2012, outearned Lady Gaga, Justin Bieber, and Rihanna to claim the title of highest-paid star under 30. The following year, the singer donated a portion of her wealth to charity by establishing the $4 million Taylor Swift Education Center at the Nashville-based Country Music Hall of Fame. Three classrooms, a learning lab, and a room with kid-friendly displays were all there when the building first opened. She said that "music education is really such an important part of my life" in an interview with CMT Hot 20 Countdown. When I learned how to play the guitar and write my own songs, which can't necessarily all be learned at school since there aren't enough hours in the day, my life changed so drastically.

According to the CMA website, Swift received the CMA Pinnacle Award in 2013 for her accomplishments as a singer of country music and for her "positive impact" on the genre. At the CMA Awards event that November, she also took home two more honors for her work with Tim McGraw and Keith Urban. Swift won home the AMA Award for Artist of the Year for the third time in a row at the American Music Awards, adding to her string of victories.

DISCOGRAPHY

2006: Taylor Swift.

2008: Fearless.

2010: Speak Now.

2012: Red.

2014: 1989.

2017: Reputation

FILMOGRAPHY

2009: Jonas Brothers: The 3D Concert Experience.

2009: Hannah Montana: The Movie.

2010: Valentine's Day.

2012: The Lorax /Voz.

2014: The Giver.

TOURS

2009-2010: Fearless Tour.

2011-2012: Speak Now World Tour.

2013-2014: Red Tour.

2015: The 1989 World Tour.

TELEVISION

2009: CSI: Crime Scene Investigation
Episode: "Turn, Turn, Turn"

2013: New Girl Episode: "Elaine's Big Day".

QUOTES

I am a person that can do a lot, and I want to be recognized for the positive things I have accomplished in my life.

If you constantly reflect on yesterday, you cannot have a better future.

Even if I am far away, I won't abandon you.

There are several little setbacks in life.

Not fall in love, but love. As a result of everything falling, I am a person that can do a lot, and I want to be recognized for the positive things I have accomplished in my life.

If you constantly reflect on yesterday, you cannot have a better future.

Even if I am far away, I won't abandon you.

There are several little setbacks in life.

Not fall in love, but love. As a result of everything falling,

when did she become famous

Taylor Swift's rise to fame: how? Taylor Swift signed a song publishing contract with Sony/ATV at the age of 14, becoming the Records' youngest signing in the company's history and scoring her first Top 40 hit. Swift joined Big Machine in 2006

Taylors fans

Taylor Swift's followers go under the appellation of Swifties. The name is derived from the name "Swift," simply. It's a moniker that sets Taylor Swift supporters apart from other fan bases.

Taylor swift Net worth

Taylor Swift's net worth in 2023 is up to $570 million, according to Forbes. While other outlets such as Celebrity Net Worth and Wealthy Gorilla put her at $400 million, Forbes notes a huge jump from 2020 to 2021 to put her at $550 million, with then another jump to get to $570 million and climbing.

CHAPTER SIX: Taylor Swift tour 2023: Full schedule, dates, where to buy tickets

Beginning on March 17 in Glendale, Arizona, Taylor Swift's tour will culminate on August 9 in Los Angeles, California.

Swifties, Taylor Swift is finally ready to perform live.

On March 17 in Glendale, Arizona, Swift will begin her tour, which will culminate on August 9 in Los Angeles, California.

Swift will perform three performances in Philadelphia from May 12–14 and three in East Rutherford, New Jersey at MetLife Stadium from May 26–28.

A few of the eagerly awaited opening artists for "The Eras Tour" include Paramore, Haim, Gayle, Girl in Red, Beebadoobee, Pheobe Bridgers, Muna, Gracie Abrams, and Owenn.

Swift's countrywide tour will include 44 performances in all.

The expense of many shows is still astronomical, with some tickets reaching $2,000 or more. Over the next weeks, fans will likely search the secondary market in the hopes that the price will fall.

Here is a list of all of Taylor Swift's U.S. tour dates, along with links to secondary market and resale ticketing websites.

Glendale, Arizona (March 17)

Tickets: StubHub | TicketNetwork | Vivid Seats

Glendale, Arizona (March 18)

Tickets: StubHub | TicketNetwork | Vivid Seats

Las Vegas, Nevada (March 24)

Tickets: StubHub | TicketNetwork | Vivid Seats

Las Vegas, Nevada (March 25)

Tickets: StubHub | TicketNetwork | Vivid Seats

Arlington, Texas (March 31)

Tickets: StubHub | TicketNetwork | Vivid Seats

Arlington, Texas (April 1)

Tickets: StubHub | TicketNetwork | Vivid Seats

Arlington, Texas (April 2)

Tickets: StubHub | TicketNetwork | Vivid Seats

Tampa, Florida (April 13)

Tickets: StubHub | TicketNetwork | Vivid Seats

Tampa, Florida (April 14)

Tickets: StubHub | TicketNetwork | Vivid Seats

Tampa, Florida (April 15)

Tickets: StubHub | TicketNetwork | Vivid Seats

Houston, Texas (April 21)

Tickets: StubHub | TicketNetwork | Vivid Seats

Houston, Texas (April 22)

Tickets: StubHub | TicketNetwork | Vivid Seats

Houston, Texas (April 23)

Tickets: StubHub | TicketNetwork | Vivid Seats

Atlanta, Georgia (April 28)

Tickets: StubHub | TicketNetwork | Vivid Seats

Atlanta, Georgia (April 29)

Tickets: StubHub | TicketNetwork | Vivid Seats

Atlanta, Georgia (April 30)

Tickets: StubHub | TicketNetwork | Vivid Seats

Nashville, Tennessee (May 5)

Tickets: StubHub | TicketNetwork | Vivid Seats

Nashville, Tennessee (May 6)

Tickets: Stub Hub | Ticket Network | Vivid Seats

Nashville, Tennessee (May 7)

Tickets: Stub Hub | Ticket Network | Vivid Seats

Philadelphia, Pennsylvania (May 12)

Tickets: Stub Hub | Ticket Network | Vivid Seats

Philadelphia, Pennsylvania (May 13)

Tickets: Stub Hub | Ticket Network | Vivid Seats

Philadelphia, Pennsylvania (May 14)

Tickets: Stub Hub | Ticket Network | Vivid Seats

Foxborough, Massachusetts (May 19)

Tickets: Stub Hub | Ticket Network | Vivid Seats

Foxborough, Massachusetts (May 20)

Tickets: StubHub | TicketNetwork | Vivid Seats

Foxborough, Massachusetts (May 21)

Tickets: StubHub | TicketNetwork | Vivid Seats

East Rutherford, New Jersey (May 26)

Tickets: StubHub | TicketNetwork | Vivid Seats

East Rutherford, New Jersey (May 27)

Tickets: StubHub | TicketNetwork | Vivid Seats

East Rutherford, New Jersey (May 28)

Tickets: StubHub | TicketNetwork | Vivid Seats

Chicago, Illinois (June 2)

Tickets: StubHub | TicketNetwork | Vivid Seats

Chicago, Illinois (June 3)

Tickets: StubHub | TicketNetwork | Vivid Seats

Chicago, Illinois (June 4)

Tickets: StubHub | TicketNetwork | Vivid Seats

Detroit, Michigan (June 9)

Tickets: StubHub | TicketNetwork | Vivid Seats

Detroit, Michigan (June 10)

Tickets: StubHub | TicketNetwork | Vivid Seats

Pittsburgh, Pennsylvania (June 16)

Tickets: StubHub | TicketNetwork | Vivid Seats

Pittsburgh, Pennsylvania (June 17)

Tickets: StubHub | TicketNetwork | Vivid Seats

Minneapolis, Minnesota (June 23)

Tickets: StubHub | TicketNetwork | Vivid Seats

Minneapolis, Minnesota (June 24)

Tickets: StubHub | TicketNetwork | Vivid Seats

Cincinnati, Ohio (June 30)

Tickets: StubHub | TicketNetwork | Vivid Seats

Cincinnati, Ohio (July 1)

Tickets: StubHub | TicketNetwork | Vivid Seats

Kansas City, Missouri (July 7)

Tickets: StubHub | TicketNetwork | Vivid Seats

Kansas City, Missouri (July 8)

Tickets: StubHub | TicketNetwork | Vivid Seats

Denver, Colorado (July 14)

Tickets: StubHub | TicketNetwork | Vivid Seats

Denver, Colorado (July 15)

Tickets: StubHub | TicketNetwork | Vivid Seats

Seattle, Washington (July 22)

Tickets: StubHub | TicketNetwork | Vivid Seats

Seattle, Washington (July 23)

Tickets: StubHub | TicketNetwork | Vivid Seats

Santa Clara, California (July 28)

Tickets: StubHub | TicketNetwork | Vivid Seats

Santa Clara, California (July 29)

Tickets: StubHub | TicketNetwork | Vivid Seats

Los Angeles, California (Aug. 3)

Tickets: StubHub | TicketNetwork | Vivid Seats

Los Angeles, California (Aug. 4)

Tickets: StubHub | TicketNetwork | Vivid Seats

Los Angeles, California (Aug. 5)

Tickets: StubHub | TicketNetwork | Vivid Seats

Los Angeles, California (Aug. 8)

Tickets: StubHub | TicketNetwork | Vivid
Seats

Los Angeles, California (Aug. 9)

Tickets: StubHub | TicketNetwork | Vivid
Seats

CHAPTER SEVEN: Taylor Swift New Album and release date

At her Nashville event, Taylor Swift launches the third album in the "Taylor's Version" series, "Speak Now (Taylor's Version)"

The third chapter of pop diva Taylor Swift's "Taylor's Version" releases, "Speak Now (Taylor's Version)," has been revealed.

Tennessee-born Swift choose her Nashville performance on Friday night to make the "Speak Now (Taylor's Version)" debut.

On July 7th, the album will be made accessible. It will be the third song from her back catalog to be re-recorded after "Red (Taylor's Version)" and "Fearless (Taylor's Version)."

Six new songs as well as updated versions of her originals will be included on the upcoming album.

The musician said, "I always looked at this album as my album, and the lump in my throat expands to a quivering voice as I say this," in a message on Twitter. Because of you, my reader, it will happen at last.

The finest thing I've ever owned is this music, together with your belief in me.

Jessye Farquharson, a huge admirer of Taylor Swift and a singer-songwriter, responded to Insider's question: "It earned honors but wasn't widely praised by reviewers, and I feel like it's not the jury favorite, but it's our favorite and has always been mine.

She reclaimed her self-written record in the city where all of her masters were stolen, so it is extra meaningful that she decided to reveal it on her first date there.

The ownership of the master recordings for her first six studio albums was the subject of a widely publicized dispute between American singer-songwriter Swift and her previous record company, Big Machine Records, its founder Scott Borchetta, and its new owner Scooter Braun in June 2019.

The original "Speak Now" album was deemed by Insider's Abigail Abesamis Demarest to be Swift's "most iconic" record, thus the remastered version has a lot to live up to.

Previous rerecorded albums by Taylor Swift have achieved enormous success, with "Red (Taylor's Version)" shattering Spotify's record for the most-streamed album by a female artist in a day on the day it was released.

CHAPTER EIGHT: fun facts about Taylor swift

Here are some of the most fascinating details about Taylor Swift, one of the greatest stars in the world. Taylor Swift has had a very successful career, rising from her modest beginnings as a small-town country singer to one of the most well-known and popular musicians of all time.

Did you know that in February 2015, Taylor Swift became the first international female solo artist to win a BRIT Award?

These interesting facts about Taylor Swift, the gorgeous, brilliant, and award-winning American singer-songwriter, will delight you if you're a fan.

She goes by Taylor Alison Swift.

Taylor Swift was born on December 13, 1989, in Reading, Pennsylvania, and is now 33 years old.

Taylor was raised on the family's Christmas tree farm, which her father had acquired from one of his customers.

Her father is Scott Kingsley Swift, and her mother is Andrea Finlay.

The University of Manoa in Hawaii was the father of Taylor's college-age children.

Because Andrea didn't want people to be able to infer her daughter's gender from her name alone, she decided to call her Taylor.

Austin, Taylor's younger brother, was a student at Vanderbilt University and a part-time freelance photographer.

Swift was influenced by her grandmother's career as a professional opera singer

Taylor has gone by several monikers throughout the years, including Tay, Swifty, T-Swift, T-Swizzle, and T-Sweezy.

Swift began performing in front of crowds at local competitions and fairs when she was ten years old.

She had a performance at a Philadelphia 76ers game when she was 11 years old, singing "The Star-Spangled Banner." She also triumphed in a local talent contest by performing "Big Deal" by LeAnn Rimes.

When Taylor was 12 years old, a computer repairman showed her how to play three chords on the guitar. This gave Taylor the idea to start playing the guitar and creating songs. The title of her first song was "Lucky You."

When Taylor was 12 years old, she authored a 350-page book that has never been released.

Taylor Swift is a very gifted musician; she is proficient on the guitar, piano, ukulele, electric guitar, and banjo.

13 is Taylor Swift's lucky number, which is unusual. She was not only born on the thirteenth day, but her first album also achieved gold status after 13 weeks and had a 13-second entrance in its opening track.

For her follow-up album Fearless, Taylor Swift won Album of the Year at the 2010 Grammy Awards, making her the youngest artist in history to do so.

Taylor Swift made history by selling more than a million copies of two albums in their first week of release with her albums Speak Now and Red.

She is a skilled painter as well.

A pair of cowboy boots is one of her favorite pieces of clothes to wear.

Her major musical inspiration, according to her, is Shania Twain, although Britney Spears also has her "devoted" support.

Taylor was inspired to go to Nashville, Tennessee after seeing a Behind the Music episode on Faith Hill.

Taylor relocated to Nashville with her family when she was 14 years old.

At the time, Taylor Swift began utilizing MySpace to grow her fan base, which was fairly unusual in the country music industry.

In an interview in 2005, a reporter said to Taylor, "If music doesn't work out, you could be a hair model." The same lady interviewed her once again in 2012 and expressed regret for expressing it.

Taylor signed a recording deal with Scott Borchetta's Big Machine Records after giving a performance at The Bluebird Care in Nashville in 2006.

She and Selena Gomez are good friends.

Tim McGraw, Taylor's first single, made it into the top 10 of the country charts in 2006.

In October 2006, Taylor launched her first album, which went on to sell over 2.5 million copies.

Cheesecake is her favorite sweet treat.

From July to October 2008, Swift dated singer Joe Jonas. Many of the songs on her Fearless album, such as "Forever and Always" and "You're Not Sorry," were about their split.

By selling over 20 million digital downloads in 2009—more than any other country artist—Taylor Swift shattered the previous record for the genre.

In 2009, Taylor portrayed a disobedient kid named Haley Jones in an episode of CSI. Out of admiration for the program, Taylor also created a CSI remix of her song "You're Not Sorry."

Late in 2009, Taylor dated actor Taylor Lautner, who became well-known for his part in the Twilight Saga.

Taylor only wears her spectacles while she's at home and doesn't use her contact lenses.

Swift has an eight-bedroom vacation home in Watch Hill, Rhode Island, near the shore.

Additionally, she owns an airfield hangar at Nashville International airfield as well as a Dassault Falcon 900 private plane!

She enjoys reading To Kill A Mockingbird among other works.

She played Felicia in the 2010 movie Valentine's Day.

Swift was voted Woman of the Year by Billboard in 2011!

Taylor received "The Big Help Award" in 2012 from Lady Michelle Obama in recognition of her commitment to helping others.

In The Lorax, she provided the voice for the Audrey character.

From late 2012 to January 2013, she was romantically linked to One Direction singer Harry Styles.

She played Elaine in a 2013 episode of New Girl.

Taylor requested her followers to appear in the Shake it Off music video with professional dancers.

Taylor also as Rosemary in the 2014 movie version of The Giver.

Taylor's fifth studio album, 1989, was made available to the public on October 27, 2014, through Big Machine Records.

Swift gathered 89 of her best admirers to her home to listen to 1989 before it was released; Taylor also made cookies for her visitors.

2014's best-selling album was 1989, surpassing the Frozen soundtrack from Disney. I can't thank you enough for helping 1989 become the best-selling album of 2014, she tweeted on New Year's Eve. NOW LETS GO CELEBRATE!"

A 4-year-old child with terminal brain cancer was able to check off her last bucket list item—"to dance to Shake it off with Tay Tay"—thanks to Taylor Swift. When she saw #ShakeItOffJalene trending on Twitter, she called the girl to set up a FaceTime call.

In February 2015, she took home her first BRIT Award for International Female Solo Artist.

@taylorswift13 is her Twitter handle.

You'd have to be insane not to love Taylor Swift.

We knew she was trouble from the beginning, and you couldn't possibly brush it off.

Taylor Swift has a long list of number-one singles under her belt and has helped many people, including a young person with terminal brain cancer.

Swift and Big Machine Records agreed to a 13-year recording deal in 2005. Her breakthrough song, "Tim McGraw," was subsequently released before she released her self-titled debut album. Swift's self-titled album would later become popular, selling 7.27 million copies globally. The album has also received at least four Platinum certifications from the RIAA as of this writing.

Swift followed up her great album debut with another smash song, Fearless. The second album has some of Swift's most well-known songs, including "Love Story" and "You Belong With Me." The song Fearless would go on to reach the top of several music charts and receive Platinum certification internationally. In fact, Fearless ultimately earned a Diamond certification in the US. More than 11.9 million copies of the album have been sold worldwide, making it Swift's second-best-selling album overall.

Swift proceeded to solidify her position as perhaps the finest female solo country-pop singer of her age after releasing successful songs and albums. She released popular albums like Red and Speak Now. Her most popular album, 1989, was released in 2014.

Top hits from 1989 include "Blank Space," "Bad Blood," "Shake It Off," and many more. Over 14.3 million copies of the record would eventually be sold. With "Shake It Off" and Fearless, Swift became the first solo female artist to have a Diamond single and album.

Swift's sixth album, Reputation, which would be her last on Big Machine Records, was released in 2017. Swift reached her breaking point when Scooter Braun's Ithaca Holdings paid $300 million for the publication rights to six of her albums. Swift finally acquired publication rights to all six of her albums after a certain amount of time since she was the primary songwriter of all of her songs. She also moved to Republic Records, in addition.

Despite the continuous public spat between Swift and Big Machine Records, Swift's career as a musician flourished with Republic Records. Her discography includes the albums Lover, Folklore, and Evermore. Lover became Swift's sixth album to sell at least 500,000 copies in a week with sales of 867,000 equivalent album units in a week. Swift is the first female musician to do this.

In 2021, Swift re-recorded a few of her prior popular songs with the addition of "Taylor's Version" once the disagreement was handled as promised. Swift's reissues were warmly welcomed by both her admirers and her detractors. In reality, in terms of overall album sales in 2021, her re-released albums Red (Taylor's Version) and Fearless (Taylor's Version) would come in second and fourth, respectively.

Swift's tenth studio album, Midnights, was released in 2022. With 1.578 million equivalent album units sold, Midnights would go on to become the fastest-selling album in the United States. With the success of Midnights, Swift tied Barbra Streisand for the most number one albums by a female artist with her 11th album at the top of the Billboard 200 list.

Swift's music business, including sales of her albums, gigs, and merchandise, accounts for the majority of her net worth. Swift has really earned more than $150 million from her several tours, including the very successful 1989 global tour and Reputation stadium tour. The Eras Tour, which will be her sixth headlining concert tour and will honor all of her albums, is the upcoming event. This tour has generated significant controversy due to outrageous ticket pricing and the Ticketmaster debacle,

Taylor Swift is the first and only female solo artist to have three solo albums win the Grammy for Album of the Year.

4. Taylor Swift has 58 Guinness World Records under her belt!

She has several incredible records, such as:

Most Popular Online Music Video (Female Artist) for "Shake It Off."

The single "We Are Never Getting Back Together" sold the most copies in digital history.

'Look What You Made Me Do' was the most streamed song on Spotify in the first 24 hours.

5. Taylor Swift and Ed Sheeran are close friends!

.

Even their songs "Everything has Changed" and "The Joker and The Queen" were written together.

The term "Swifties" is used by Taylor Swift supporters. The moniker was allegedly created by a fan and is based on Taylor's last name.

Swifties are among of Taylor's most devoted supporters and are regarded as some of the finest!

7. Universities provide courses on Taylor Swift!

The career and cultural significance of Taylor are the subject of a course at the Clive Davis Institute in New York!

Imagine spending an hour listening to Taylor after math class at school; we wouldn't be upset.

8. One of the most giving celebs is Taylor Swift.

.

She is widely recognized for giving millions of dollars to a variety of charitable organizations, including disaster relief money and the music programs at six US institutions!

She supports children's reading and has given money and books to schools around the nation to enhance education. Perhaps we ought to enroll her in Fun Kids Book Worms?

9. Taylor Swift has 47.3 million YouTube followers.

The 38th most subscribed YouTube channel in the world is hers, where she publishes her music videos.

10. There have been 27 Taylor Swift songs that can be recognized from their lyrics in one minute.

CHAPTER NINE: Taylor swifts song and Album Taylor swifts song and Album

With the release of her self-titled album in 2006, Taylor Swift debuted on the country music scene. Since then, she has won over fans everywhere with her musical and lyrical prowess. Taylor Swift released three country albums before beginning the stunning and flawless move to pop with her fourth studio album, Red.

With her most recent albums, folklore and evermore, she even ventured into the alternative and folk genres, adding to her varied repertoire of accessible hits. She now has three pure pop albums to her credit. She is presently adding new songs to her older albums, starting with Fearless, and re-releasing them to better diversify her discography.

The ability of Taylor Swift's words to captivate her audience has always been one of her best talents. She is broadly attractive across genres because to the resonant themes of love, loss, and heartache that appear in many of her songs. Swifties, as Taylor Swift's fans are known, believe that the singer is putting their own experiences into words so they can sing along at the top of their lungs.

Every song that has ever appeared on a Taylor Swift album is her own composition. On some, she collaborates with established and brand-new writing partners; on others, she works alone. She collaborates closely with producers to create the finest tunes possible.

Learn more about each Taylor Swift album, including its release date, track listing, singles, and sources of musical inspiration, in the sections below.

Table of contents for Taylor Swift's albums, listed by date of release:

Taylor Swift Albums

Fearless

Speak Now

Speak Now World Tour – Live

Red

1989

Reputation

Lover

folklore

evermore

Taylor Swift albums in order

The following are Taylor Swift albums in order of release date.

'Taylor Swift'

Release Date: October 24, 2006

Versions: Regular, 2008 Reissue, Best Buy Digital Download, Deluxe

Taylor swifts' Track lists

Taylor Swift Tracklist:

1. Tim McGraw

2. Picture To Burn

3. Teardrops On My Guitar

4. A Place In This World

5. Cold As You

6. The Outside

7. Tied Together With A Smile

8. Stay Beautiful

9. Should've Said No

10. Mary's Song (Oh My My My)

11. Our Song

12. I'm Only Me When I'm With You (2008, Deluxe)

13. Invisible (2008, Deluxe)

14. A Perfectly Good Heart (2008, Deluxe)

15. Teardrops on My Guitar Pop Version (2008)

16. Taylor Swift's first phone call with Tim McGraw (Deluxe)

17. I Heart ? (Best Buy Digital Download)

When Taylor Swift released her first album at the age of only 16, the record quickly rocked the world of country music. The record included breakup ballads like "Picture to Burn" and "Should've Said No," serious love songs like "Tim McGraw," "Mary's Song," and the very popular "Our Song," as well as the profound, far-beyond-her-years "Cold As You," which was the first of Swift's illustrious "Track 5s." Check out this post rating all of these tunes for additional information!

The label that would go on to collaborate with Taylor for her next five albums, Big Machine Records, released the record, which was entirely produced by Nathan Chapman.

The first time we encountered Taylor Swift's infamous penchant for easter eggs was on the CD liner. With the exception of a few strategically placed capital letters, she kept the song's purpose hidden in the lyrics. The song's inspiration was revealed by the uppercase letters. See them listed below.

. Tim McGraw – Can't tell me nothin'

2. Picture To Burn – Date nice boys

3. Teardrops On My Guitar – He will never know

4. A Place In This World – Found it

5. Cold As You – Time to let go

6. The Outside – You are not alone

7. Tied Together With A Smile – You are loved

8. Stay Beautiful – Shake N' Bake

9. Should've Said No – Sam Sam Sam Sam Sam Sam

10. Mary's Song (Oh My My My) – Sometimes love is forever

11. Our Song – Live in love

When "Tim McGraw" was released as the album's first single, Swift was instantly propelled to a level of stardom that few people ever reach. The song earned platinum certification, as did the album's next four singles.

The title of the song would raise a lot of suspicions about Taylor Swift's connection with Tim McGraw, a country music singer of whom she was a major admirer. During the course of this album's tour, she went on to open for McGraw and his wife, Faith Hill, and subsequently recorded a song together called "The Highway Don't Care."

The next two singles from the album were "Teardrops on My Guitar" and "Our Song." Taylor Swift started to gain some crossover popularity with pop audiences when "Our Song" and "Teardrops" both achieved platinum status.

The last two singles released by Taylor Swift were "Picture to Burn" and "Should've Said No." Although they both achieved double platinum status, they eventually accomplished something far more significant for the artist. They enhanced her reputation among Swifties as the breakup anthem king! She created a live acoustic video for the song instead of her customary highly polished one with the latter.

'Fearless'

taylor swift, fearless

Release Date: November 11, 2008, April 9
2021

Versions: Regular, Platinum, Taylor's
Version

Fearless Tracklist:

1. Fearless

2. Fifteen

3. Love Story

4. Hey Stephen

5. White Horse

6. You Belong With Me

7. Breathe (feat. Colbie Caillat)

8. Tell Me Why

9. You're Not Sorry

10. The Way I Loved You

11. Forever & Always

12. The Best Day

13. Change

14. Jump Then Fall (Platinum)

15. Untouchable (Platinum)

16. Forever & Always – Piano Version (Platinum)

17. Come In With The Rain (Platinum)

18. Superstar (Platinum)

19. The Other Side Of The Door (Platinum)

20. Today Was a Fairytale (Taylor's Version)

21. You All Over Me (feat. Maren Morris) (Taylor's Version)

22. Mr. Perfectly Fine (Taylor's Version)

23. We Were Happy (Taylor's Version)

24. That's When (feat. Keith Urban) (Taylor's Version)

25. Don't You (Taylor's Version)

26. Bye Bye Baby (Taylor's Version)

Taylor Swift added the distinction of co-producer to her portfolio with Fearless! She and Nathan Chapman co-produced each song on her sophomore album.

This is not the sophomore slump! Taylor Swift continued to weave tales about love and heartache on her second album, and she was becoming better at it. Taylor Swift kept her country followers from her debut while gaining more and more pop admirers with her album Fearless, which was categorized as a country-pop album.

In addition, Fearless would go on to become the album with the most awards in the history of country music, giving Taylor Swift her first Grammy for "Album of the Year" among many other honors. Additionally, it had outstanding commercial success, earning certified diamond status.

Swifties' devotion with their beloved star began with the album Fearless. She started hanging out with and even dating other prominent individuals after becoming well-known thanks to her first record. And Taylor Swift will unavoidably create a song about dating at some time in the future! Fans believe that Swift's song "Forever & Always" is about Joe Jonas, whom she dated for a short while until he supposedly dumped her during the course of a 27-second phone conversation.

Related: 8 lessons I learned from Taylor Swift's Fearless about love and life

Taylor Swift re-recorded and published her debut album, Fearless, in order to reclaim control of her works. On April 9, 2021, she released Fearless (Taylor's Version), which included six all-new songs as well as "Today Was a Fairytale," a song that had previously only been featured on the soundtrack for the movie Valentine's Day, in which she had a supporting role.

Check out the liner note hints for Taylor Swift's Fearless for additional song meanings. There were no hints in the liner notes for the tracks that were released with (Taylor's Version).

1. Fearless - I loved you before we ever met 2. Fifteen - I sobbed while recording this 3. Love Story - Someday I'll discover this 4. Hey Stephen - Love and stealing

5. White Horse: "All I ever wanted was the truth"

6. You Belong With Me - Love is blind, therefore you couldn't see me

7. Breathe (feat. Colbie Caillat) - I'm sorry, I'm sorry, I'm sorry 8. Tell Me Why - Guess I was duped by your grin

9. She can take you; You're Not Sorry

The Way I Loved You: We Can't Go Back

11. Forever & Always - If you play these games, we'll both lose.

12. God's blessings on The Best Day Ms. Andrea Swift

13. Change - Thanks to you, things have changed for me.

14. Jump Then Fall (Platinum) - The previous summer was fantastic.

15. Untouchable (Platinum) - We constantly seek what we can't have.

16. Forever & Always - Piano Version (Platinum) - I still mourn the person I thought he was 17. Come In With The Rain (Platinum) - I won't say I wish you'd come back.

18. SuperStar (Platinum): "I'll never tell."
19. "The Other Side Of The Door" (Platinum): "What I was really thinking when I slammed the door."

All of the singles on Fearless reached at least certified platinum status, much like Taylor Swift. The cute and still-loved "Love Story," which borrows elements from Romeo & Juliet, served as the first single from Fearless. The music video starts with Taylor Swift admiring the guy she loves at school and concludes with her in a princess gown engaged in a passionate love affair with the same boy.

The next track, "White Horse," is the second of Taylor Swift's well-known Track 5 songs. It employs fairytale motifs to discuss love and sorrow, much as "Love Story," too.

The next song from the album, "You Belong With Me," became infamous for all the wrong reasons. Kanye West reportedly interrupted Taylor Swift on stage when she was winning the MTV Video Music Award for "Best Female Video," claiming that "Beyonce had one of the best videos of all time." Following this episode, the two celebrities began an ongoing, on-and-off enmity that has lasted more than ten years.

"Fifteen" and "Fearless," which were the album's last two singles, were performed by Taylor Swift. With intimate information about Swift and her closest friend, Abigal, "Fifteen" delves into a young girl's high school experience, while "Fearless" explores one of the many great experiences you get while falling in love. The "Fearless" music video features scenes from Swift's tour, which changed her life.

The next track, "White Horse," is the second of Taylor Swift's well-known Track 5 songs. It employs fairytale motifs to discuss love and sorrow, much as "Love Story," too.

The next song from the album, "You Belong With Me," became infamous for all the wrong reasons. Kanye West reportedly interrupted Taylor Swift on stage when she was winning the MTV Video Music Award for "Best Female Video," claiming that "Beyonce had one of the best videos of all time." Following this episode, the two celebrities began an ongoing, on-and-off enmity that has lasted more than ten years.

"Fifteen" and "Fearless," which were the album's last two singles, were performed by Taylor Swift. With intimate information about Swift and her closest friend, Abigal, "Fifteen" delves into a young girl's high school experience, while "Fearless" explores one of the many great experiences you get while falling in love. The "Fearless" music video features scenes from Swift's tour, which changed her life.

'Speak Now'

Release Date: October 25, 2010

Versions: Regular, Deluxe

Speak Now Tracklist:

1. Mine

2. Sparks Fly

3. Back To December

4. Speak Now

5. Dear John

6. Mean

7. The Story Of Us

8. Never Grow Up

9. Enchanted

10. Better Than Revenge

11. Innocent

12. Haunted

13. Last Kiss

14. Long Live

15. Ours (Deluxe)

16. If This Was A Movie (Deluxe)

17. Superman (Deluxe)

18. Back To December – Acoustic Version (Deluxe)

19. Haunted – Acoustic Version (Deluxe)

20. Mine – POP Mix (Deluxe)

The second country-pop album Taylor Swift and Nathan Chapman collaborated on is titled Speak Now. The album had several subjects that were more adult, such as Taylor Swift's relationship with John Mayer, who was 12 years older, and the Kanye West and Kanye West VMA controversy.

However, Speak Now also included a lot of Taylor Swift's trademark storytelling in the form of the utterly "awww"-worthy "Mine," "Enchanted," and "Never Grow Up," as well as the anti-bullying anthem, "Mean," and one of Swift's most incisive and delectably petty works to date, "Better Than Revenge."

Some of Taylor Swift's more graphic hints may be found in the Speak Now liner notes. In "Back to December," "Enchanted," and "Innocent," she specifically names out Taylor Lautner and Owl City's Adam Young, and she didn't even bother to exclude John Mayer's name from the credits! She included that right in the heading. This may be an indication of the increased amount of power she was experiencing as a consequence of receiving constant criticism.

Check out all of the Speak Now album liner clues here.

1. Mine – Toby

2. Sparks Fly – Portland Oregon

3. Back To December – Tay

4. Speak Now – You always regret what you don't say

5. Dear John – Loved you from the very first day

6. Mean – I thought you got me

7. The Story Of Us – CMT awards

8. Never Grow Up – I moved out in July

9. Enchanted – Adam

10. Better Than Revenge – You thought I would forget

11. Innocent – Life is full of little interruptions

12. Haunted – Still to this day

13. Last Kiss – Forever and always

14. Long Live – For you

There were an astounding six singles on Speak Now, all of which achieved platinum certification. The album's first hit, "Mine," is a reverie about a possible love tale that Swift let escape

One of Swift's earliest songs, "Back to December," which describes a moment when she screwed up and lost a terrific person, is one of her rawest and most sincere works. namely Taylor Lautner.

Taylor Swift's subsequent music videos for "Mean" and "Speak Now" are among her most entertaining and memorable ones, showcasing her love of costumes.

"Ours" and "Sparks Fly" marked the end of Taylor Swift's Speak Now phase. "Ours" is one of the loveliest love songs and videos on the album, while "Sparks Fly" is another live performance showcasing highlights from the tour!

Speak Now World Tour – Live Tracklist:

1. Sparks Fly

2. Mine

3. The Story of Us

4. Mean

5. Ours

6. Back to December/Apologize/You're Not Sorry

7. Better than Revenge

8. Speak Now

9. Last Kiss

10. Drops of Jupiter

11. Bette Davis Eyes

12. I Want You Back

13. Dear John

14. Enchanted

15. Haunted

16. Long Live

Additionally, a live CD from Taylor Swift's Speak Now tour was published. All of the songs from the album are included, along with a fantastic mashup of "Back to December," "Apologize," and "You're Not Sorry," as well as renditions of "Bette Davis Eyes," "Train's "Drops of Jupiter," and "I Want You Back" by the Jackson 5 and Kim Carnes.

Red'

taylor swift album guide

Release Date: October 22, 2012

Versions: Regular, Deluxe Red'

taylor swift album guide

Release Date: October 22, 2012

Versions: Regular, Deluxe

Red Tracklist:

1. State of Grace

2. Red

3. Treacherous

4. I Knew You Were Trouble

5. All Too Well

6. 22

7. I Almost Do

8. We Are Never Ever Getting Back Together

9. Stay Stay Stay

10. The Last Time (feat. Gary Lightbody)

11. Holy Ground

12. Sad Beautiful Tragic

13. The Lucky One

14. Everything Has Changed (feat. Ed Sheeran)

15. Starlight

16. Begin Again

17. The Moment I Knew (Deluxe)

18. Come Back...Be Here (Deluxe)

19. Girl At Home (Deluxe)

20. Treacherous – Original Demo Recording (Deluxe)

21. Red – Original Demo Recording (Deluxe)

22. State of Grace – Acoustic Version (Deluxe

The song of the same name does a very good job at encapsulating Red. The album is about "red" love. fierce, ardent, and powerful. The album combines many genres from song to song to provide a phenomenally powerful mix of tunes that practically any music listener may enjoy.

Taylor Swift and Nathan Chapman jointly produced Red, which was her most "pop"-oriented album to date. Nevertheless, tracks like "Red," "Holy Ground," and "Begin Again" keep the album rooted in the country origins of the artist.

With this album, Taylor Swift's songwriting and narrative were at their most in-depth. Her music was becoming better and better as it became apparent that she was maturing and starting to experience things in a more mature and nuanced manner.

Liner notes for the album include explicit mentions to Taylor Swift's ex-boyfriend Conor Kennedy in the songs "Everything Has Changed" and "Starlight." Swift and Kennedy were seen on camera sharing a kiss at Hyannis Port, and Ethel is Conor's grandma.

Many tracks on this album, including "We Are Never Ever Getting Back Together" and "All Too Well," which is still one of Swifties' favorite and most beautiful songs, are said to be about Jake Gyllenhaal. With "I Knew You Were Trouble," Harry Styles is also certain to get an early nomination.

1. State of Grace – I love you doesn't count after goodbye

2. Red – SAG

3. Treacherous – Won't stop till it's over

4. I Knew You Were Trouble – When you saw me dancing

5. All Too Well – Maple Latte

6. 22 – Ashley Dianna Claire Selena

7. I Almost Do – Wrote this instead of calling

8. We Are Never Ever Getting Back Together – When I stopped caring what you thought

9. Stay Stay Stay – Daydreaming about real love

10. The Last Time (feat. Gary Lightbody) – LA on your break

11. Holy Ground – When you came to the show in SD

12. Sad Beautiful Tragic – While you were on a train

13. The Lucky One – Wouldn't you like to know

14. Everything Has Changed (feat. Ed Sheeran) – Hyannis Port

15. Starlight – For Ethel

16. Begin Again – I wear heels now

1989'

Release Date: October 27, 2014

Versions: Regular, Deluxe

1989 Tracklist:

1. Welcome to New York

2. Blank Space

3. Style

4. Out of the Woods

5. All You Had to Do Was Stay

6. Shake It Off

7. I Wish You Would

8. Bad Blood

9. Wildest Dreams

10. How You Get the Girl

11. This Love

12. I Know Places

13. Clean

14. Wonderland (Deluxe)

15. You Are In Love (Deluxe)

16. New Romantics (Deluxe)

17. I Know Places – Voice Memo (Deluxe)

18. I Wish You Would – Voice Memo (Deluxe)

19. Blank Space – Voice Memo (Deluxe)

1989, Taylor Swift's first full-length pop album, marked her official entry into the mainstream music industry. While maintaining Nathan Chapman on her new production team, she also collaborated with a broad range of renowned industry greats, such as Ryan Tedder, Jack Antonoff, Max Martin, and Shellback.

Taylor Swift received her second Grammy for "Album of the Year" with 1989. She has said that she intended each song on 1989 to embody the themes it explored. This was expertly accomplished by her using songs like the frenzied "Out of the Woods," the chill "Style," the hopeless "I Wish You Would," and the energizing "Clean."

For 1989, the record liner notes operated a bit differently, delivering a whole tale instead of providing discrete hints. Because the album mostly tells the narrative of one love affair—possibly between Taylor Swift and Harry Styles—fans assume that this is the case. There are several overt indications that Harry is involved, such as the song "Style" and references to his distinctive paper aircraft necklace. 1989, Taylor Swift's first full-length pop album, marked her official entry into the mainstream music industry. While maintaining Nathan Chapman on her new production team, she also collaborated with a broad range of renowned industry greats, such as Ryan Tedder, Jack Antonoff, Max Martin, and Shellback.

Taylor Swift received her second Grammy for "Album of the Year" with 1989. She has said that she intended each song on 1989 to embody the themes it explored. This was expertly accomplished by her using songs like the frenzied "Out of the Woods," the chill "Style," the hopeless "I Wish You Would," and the energizing "Clean."

For 1989, the record liner notes operated a bit differently, delivering a whole tale instead of providing discrete hints. Because the album mostly tells the narrative of one love affair—possibly between Taylor Swift and Harry Styles—fans assume that this is the case. There are several overt indications that Harry is involved, such as the song "Style" and references to his distinctive paper aircraft necklace.

Check out the album liner notes for 1989 here.

1. Welcome to New York – We begin our story in New York

2. Blank Space – There once was a girl known by everyone and no one

3. Style – Her heart belonged to someone who couldn't stay

4. Out of the Woods – They loved each other recklessly

5. All You Had to Do Was Stay – They paid the price

6. Shake It Off – She danced to forget him

7. I Wish You Would – He drove past her street each night

8. Bad Blood – She made friends and enemies

9. Wildest Dreams – He only saw her in his dreams

10. How You Get the Girl – Then one day he came back

11. This Love – Timing is a funny thing

12. I Know Places – And everyone was watching

13. Clean – She lost him but she found herself and somehow that was everything

1989 had seven singles, matching Red. She opened with the dance-inducing "Shake It Off," giving the impression that she was stomping off all of the media criticism she was starting to get.

Style and Blank Space were her next moves. A song about the person the media portrays her to be and one about an enduring love.

The harsh song "Bad Blood," which is purportedly about Swift's dispute with Katy Perry, came next for the 1989 period. Some of Taylor Swift's backup dancers defected to perform on Katy Perry's tour, which is said to be the root of the dispute. Numerous of Swift's most well-known acquaintances, including Selena Gomez, Karlie Kloss, Hailee Steinfeld, and Lena Dunham, may be seen in the music video.

1989 was summed up by the films "Wildest Dreams," "Out of the Woods," and "New Romantics". The final liner notes for the album are included in the "Out of the Woods" video. "She lost him, but found herself, and somehow that was everything." The tale is largely over now, but the tour-based "New Romantics" was a fun extra!

'Reputation'

Release Date: November 10, 2017

Reputation Tracklist:

1. ...Ready For it?

2. End Game (feat. Ed Sheeran and Future)

3. I Did Something Bad

4. Don't Blame Me

5. Delicate

6. Look What You Made Me Do

7. So It Goes...

8. Gorgeous

9. Getaway Car

10. King Of My Heart

11. Dancing With Our Hands Tied

12. Dress

13. This Is Why We Can't Have Nice Things

14. Call It What You Want

15. New Year's Day

Taylor Swift cleansed her social media and started marketing Reputation with a mysterious snake-themed video after a three-year gap between albums and an entire year in which she was mostly absent from the public eye. The song and music video for "Look What You Made Me Do," which she released shortly after, instantly informed fans that Reputation would be drastically different from 1989.

Related: Looking back at Reputation before Taylor Swift's next phase

The song includes the line "the old Taylor is dead," and both the song and the music video include scathing allusions to Kanye West, Kim Kardashian, Katy Perry, Calvin Harris, her court case for sexual assault, and the media. People anticipated a significant difference from what we had previously heard from her since she came into the Reputation period with guns blazing.

The truth is that "LWYMMD" wasn't truly that representative of the mood of Reputation, as is typical with Swift's early singles. Although there may have been a few more overt references to sex and drink in her songs, the general narrative and themes for which she is recognized remained. Beautiful songs like "Delicate," "King of My Heart," "Call It What You Want," and "New Year's Day" were included on Reputation; they belonged on any of her other albums.

Swift's last album with Big Machine Records, Reputation, was solely produced by Jack Antonoff, Max Martin, and Shellback.

With Reputation, one significant shift was that Taylor Swift ceased including hints in the album liners. She instead added a letter that suggested she had learnt from her past errors of divulging too much of herself. She intended to begin reserving certain items for herself.

Fans may still make assumptions about the subjects of Reputation's songs, of course. Many people think "Getaway Car," "This Is Why We Can't Have Nice Things," and many of the album's love songs are about the singer's current lover, Joe Alwyn. Others think "Getaway Car" is about her frenzied affair with Tom Hiddleston.

Seven singles were included on Reputation, the first of which was the previously stated "Look What You Made Me Do." The video concludes with all of the previous Taylor

Swifts acting in ways for which she has received a lot of flak.

The next song, "...Ready For It?" had Taylor Swift battling the public's opinion of her and the woman she had begun to become as a result of all the attention.

After the first two songs from Reputation, Taylor Swift mellowed down considerably. Her subsequent singles included "End Game," which featured Ed Sheeran and Future, as well as "New Year's Day," "Gorgeous," "Delicate," and "Getaway Car," all of which dealt with her signature themes of loss and love (with a dash of passion thrown in). Only "End Game" and "Delicate" were produced into videos out of all these songs.

'Lover'

Taylor swift

Release Date: August 23, 2019

Lover Tracklist:

1. I Forgot That You Existed

2. Cruel Summer

3. Lover

4. The Man

5. The Archer

6. I Think He Knows

7. Miss Americana & The Heartbreak Prince

8. Paper Rings

9. Cornelia Street

10. Death By A Thousand Cuts

11. London Boy

12. Soon You'll Get Better (feat. The Dixie Chicks)

13. False God

14. You Need To Calm Down

15. Afterglow

16. ME! (feat. Brendon Urie of Panic! At The Disco)

17. It's Nice To Have A Friend

18. Daylight

Lover, Taylor Swift's seventh studio album, is her happiest and sweetest work to date. With this well-received record, she undoubtedly succeeded in her goal of making an album on everything she liked.

Related: Taylor Swift's Lover demonstrates that you don't have to be broken to make history

With a few exceptions that we'll discuss with the songs, she maintained the Repuation practice of not giving any indications in the liner notes, but we may infer that a significant portion of the album is about her current lover, Joe Alwyn!

Taylor Swift's first studio album with Republic Records is titled "Lover." She now has ownership of all of the master recordings of her songs under her new deal. When she originally signed with Big Machine, a company with whom Taylor Swift has had "bad blood" in the past, they recently sold the rights to her masters to Scooter Braun. She has been extremely outspoken about how she regrets not having that choice at that time.

Taylor Swift collaborated with co-producers Joel Little and Jack Antonoff on the album Lover.

Lover currently has four singles. The first was "ME!" which graphically transformed the serpent from the Reputation period into delicate butterflies. The video, which also stars Brendon Urie from Panic! at the Disco, is full of color, cats, and cowboy boots—basically everything that defines Taylor Swift!

The next Lover single, "You Need to Calm Down," saw Taylor Swift extending her first-ever political remark, which was in reference to the Equality Act. In addition to telling naysayers they "need to calm down," the video also encourages viewers to sign the Equality Act and only features performers who identify as LGBTQ+.

The title tune from the album, "Lover," was the following single. Each room in the home shown in the music video is decorated to represent one of her past albums. In one music video, a wonderful love tale is told.

In "The Man," the album's closing track, Taylor Swift imagines what life might be like if she had adopted a man's persona instead of a woman's. In the film, she assumes a man's attire and behaves in ways that highlight the many social distinctions between men and women.

Related: Taylor Swift's "The Man" music video's five most relatable scenes folklore'

taylor swift, folklore

Release Date: July 24, 2020

Versions: Regular, Deluxe, Long Pond
Studio Sessions

Folklore Tracklist:

1. The 1

2. Cardigan

3. the last great american dynasty

4. exile (feat. Bon Iver)

5. my tears ricochet

6. mirrorball

7. seven

8. august

9. this is me trying

10. illicit affairs

11. invisible string

12. mad woman

13. epiphany

14. betty

15. peace

16. hoax

17. the lakes (Deluxe)

folklore Tracklist:

1. the 1

2. cardigan

3. the last great american dynasty

4. exile (feat. Bon Iver)

5. my tears ricochet

6. mirrorball

7. seven

8. august

9. this is me trying

10. illicit affairs

11. invisible string

12. mad woman

13. epiphany

14. betty

15. peace

16. hoax

17. the lakes (Deluxe)

The COVID-19 epidemic was still affecting the rest of the globe as Taylor Swift was writing, recording, and releasing her eighth studio album. When all hope appeared to be gone, Taylor Swift surprised her fans by releasing the album. Swifties had less than

24 hours to prepare for the release of the tiny lettered, sepia-toned, and sensuous record, as opposed to the months' worth of buildup they were accustomed to.

Taylor Swift's folklore demonstrates that she glows even brighter than her fame and her boyfriends.

Although it has been properly described to as "Red's older sister," Folklore is quite different from any of Swift's prior works and radically departs from the pop development that her previous albums had made. For 11 of the album's songs, she largely relied on "The National's" Aaron Dessner while still working with her favorite producer Jack Antonoff.

For a Disney+ special titled Folklore: The Long Pond Studio Sessions, Swift, Dessner, and Antonoff came together to perform the album live as a trio. This special's soundtrack was also made available as an album via streaming sites. Along with singing the songs, the three performers spoke about the recording process and even revealed the name of the enigmatic co-writer under the pseudonym "William Bowery" on the songs "betty" and "exile." It was actor Joe Alwyn, Swift's boyfriend, as many admirers had speculated.

Swift has divided folklore into three distinct chapters in what we hope will become a fun new tradition. These chapters on streaming sites are where the album is arranged.

'evermore'

Release Date: December 11, 2020

Versions: Regular, Deluxe

evermore Tracklist:

1. willow

2. champagne problems

3. gold rush

4. 'tis the damn season

5. tolerate it

6. no body, no crime (feat. HAIM)

7. happiness

8. dorothea

9. coney island (feat. The National)

10. ivy

11. cowboy like me

12. long story short

13. marjorie

14. closure

15. evermore (feat. Bon Iver)

16. right where you left me (Deluxe)

17. it's time to go (Deluxe evermore
Tracklist:

Taylor Swift launched her second surprise
album in 2020, evermore, with less than a
day's warning and two days before her 31st
birthday. As if one surprise album release in
2020 wasn't more than Swifties could take,
she struck again.

Evermore is well worthy of its description as
"folklore's sister record," as stated by Swift.
After folklore was finished, she apparently
simply couldn't stop writing great songs
with Aaron Dessner, so she chose not to! On
all but one of the album's tracks, he is given
credit. The exception is "Gold Rush," which
was created by Jack Antonoff. A.K.A.
"William Bowery" Joe Alwyn, who cowrote
"champagne problems," "coney island," and
"evermore" with Swift, also made a
comeback for "evermore."

35 Taylor Swift lines from "Evermore" that we'll never get tired of hearing...

Evermore is Taylor Swift's most collaborative album to date in terms of included musicians. The HAIM sisters, who have been her longtime friends, joined her for the song "no body, no crime," which is Taylor Swift's cover of The Chicks' "Goodbye Earl," Bon Iver made a comeback to appear on "evermore

CHAPTER TEN: Taylor Swift: Pop's $570 million woman

I have a cake from Swift. She refers to it as "pumpkin loaf" and describes it as looking like Jamaican ginger cake. It is placed inside a linen pouch bag that she also fashioned and embroidered with a wooden spoon cartoon. 'And I thought there'd be nothing homely for you here in a strange country,' she says, knowing that I'm seeing her at a Beverly Hills café (without any PR, management, or security involved) and that I'm alone and 6,000 miles from home.

In 2013, 23-year-old Swift is not only the most successful young pop star on Earth, a consistent Guinness World Record breaker with an estimated net worth of $220 million (£143 million), but also an accomplished baker and craftswoman (and the kind of celebrity, uniquely, who woos reporters with gifts). She stands at 5 feet 11 inches and is warm, intelligent, and vintage stylish while wearing a strawberry-print dress and winged eyeliner. She reflects on the life lessons she has learned while eating pretzels.

The public impression requires a "yeah, but," she argues, "if you reach a certain point where things are going very well." Like, "Yeah, but I hear she's crazy," or "Yeah, but she's apparently been on a lot of dates." Being a woman has a lot to do with it. I object to it. that if you're a successful woman, there must be a drawback to your personality or lifestyle. But I have no power over it. Only the music I create and how I conduct myself are within my control. Keep your attention on leading a respectable life. What's left? Insanity, if I concentrated on it. Going mad is not high on my list of priorities.

Swift's accomplishments as a composer, entrepreneur, and game-changer in the music industry surpass those of her younger self now that she is over 10 years older and recently turned 33. She has created a long list of firsts, onlys, mosts, biggests, and fastests that she is currently breaking records for. With the release of her tenth studio album, Midnights, in October, she made history by being the first performer to have ten songs rank in the top ten of the Billboard Hot 100 in its 64-year history. No male artist debuted in the Top 10 for the first time in Billboard's history.

With each successive album, she has evolved from the poet laureate of puberty to the pop-banger maestro and is now a classic singer-songwriter who continues to win over new, older admirers, like Paul McCartney, who is 80 years old. Even an academic course at New York University, taught by

Rolling Stone writer Brittany Spanos, is offered as a result of her importance.

According to Spanos, 30, whose course examines Swift via feminism, racism, politics, social media, and digital streaming, Swift "is a fascinating case study in the modern music business." The speed of change in the twenty-first century has been unexpected. And Taylor has changed along with every new development in the sector. Some people struggle to keep up.

In the era of "free" music, she has fought for musicians' financial rights, taking on Spotify (in 2014, she temporarily removed her back catalogue), Apple Music (in 2015, she protested against its free trial service that didn't pay artists; Apple then capitulated), and most notably, becoming a one-woman industry disruptor in 2019. Swift lost all control over the original recordings for her six studio albums when the label she joined at age 15—Big Machine—was sold to Scooter Braun, the manager of Justin Bieber and previously of Kanye West. Swift blasted the "tyrannical control" as "two very rich, very powerful men, using $300 million of other people's money to purchase the most feminine body of work" in a public statement.

She started re-recording her enormously popular albums after quitting the label in 2018, thus far releasing Fearless (Taylor's Version) and Red (Taylor's Version). She stipulated that she own her own masters and that Universal divide any proceeds from the sale of Spotify shares with the artists on its roster when she joined with her new label, Universal. These two demands represent significant advances in a sector that has a long history of exploitation.

The Eras Tour, her first tour in five years, tickets were published last month, however Ticketmaster had a meltdown and fans were unable to purchase them (this was attributed to "unprecedented demand" that "could have filled 900 stadiums"). Even worse, these were just the US performances; her foreign tour dates have not yet been revealed, however it is speculated that she may perform in the UK in the fall of 2023. On Instagram, Swift said that this was "excruciating." She promised to "consider how this circumstance can be improved going forward." You wouldn't bet on Ticketmaster's chances in a battle...

Taylor was intrigued by how the music business operated from a young age, according to Mark Sutherland, a former Music Week editor who is now a freelance writer based in London. And what's interesting is that she never stepped back and let her staff handle everything; she is always aware of everything that takes place in her name. She demonstrates the self-confidence of artists. Her willingness to take an active part and promote reform for a fairer business is what makes her the most influential person in music. She broadcasts these details. and is aware of her fan base's influence.

Industry lore surrounds Swift's connection with her followers. Her on-tour meet and greets, which may last up to 13 hours, are renowned. She has also hosted private listening events for groups of Swifties, or superfans, at which she personally invited individuals and sourced them from social media.

'The joke with being a Taylor Swift fan,' says Zack Hourihane, AKA The Swiftologist, a Singaporean residing in New York who runs a Swift-focused YouTube channel and podcast, 'is that you feel like you're a part of the world's most secret society.' Being an obsessive since early youth, he went to a covert listening party in 2017 after signing a 12-page non-disclosure agreement that prohibited him from discussing the specifics of the one-on-one interviews Swift delivers to everyone. He remarks, "She is so disarming." She will enquire about you, look you in the eye, and grasp your hand. She is both the most well-known person in the world and your dearest friend.

Hourihane, 26, believes that she is the architect of a Swiftian "multiverse," enticing others to participate. As an example, he uses the development of her power ballad "All Too Well," a little-known five-minute album cut from 2012's Red. Swift wrote the words to "And you call me up again just to break me like a promise/So casually cruel in the name of being honest" when she was 21. The song originally lasted 10 minutes.

She asked her audience what song they wanted to see her play at the 2014 Grammys. Red had a lot of successes, but "All Too Well" was the song that everyone desired, according to Hourihane. We kept banging it into Taylor's brain until she realized it was one of her best songs ever. When we interact with her, she reacts.

It benefits both parties. Years after Swifties cried out for it, "All Too Well (10 Minute Version)" broke the record for the longest song to ever top the Billboard charts in 2021, unseating Don McLean's "American Pie," which had held it since 1972. The song's 15-minute music video, which Swift wrote, produced, and directed with an all-female cast, won three MTV Video Music Awards (VMAs) this year: Video of the Year, Best Longform Video, and Best Direction.

Taylor Alison Swift, who was born in Pennsylvania in 1989 to Scott, a Merrill Lynch stockbroker, and Andrea, a marketing professional, always had two core beliefs: that she would succeed as a singer-songwriter, and that it was crucial to be a "good person." She was an outcast at school, banished for being "weird and different," and music gave her comfort and motivation. She began performing in musical theater at the age of nine, picked up the guitar at 12, recorded cover versions of Dolly Parton songs, and began composing her own music at the age of 13.

She convinced her parents to relocate from their suburban home to Nashville when she was 14 and had already signed her first artist development agreement, along with her younger brother Austin, in order to support her more achievable goals. She was a positive adolescent with lofty goals who was nevertheless generally adolescent, romantically idealistic, and plagued by body concerns (already counting calories at 13). Swift acknowledged that she was a "intrinsically insecure" artist who lived for approval in the lauded 2020 documentary Miss Americana, but that doing so came at a high cost: "If that's where you derive all of your joy and fulfillment, one bad thing can cause everything to crumble." She said, "Most of my learning and most of my strength were developed in those times.

The more famous you are, the more of a target you become. Swift's astronomically successful career was derailed first in 2009, when she was only 19 years old. Swift's victory speech at the VMAs was interrupted by Kanye West, the world's trendiest rapper at the time, who proclaimed Beyoncé's song "Single Ladies" the winner. Swift thought the lengthy booing as he departed the stage were directed at her.

As the following decade progressed, she gained notoriety on a stadium-level, and the tabloids regularly made fun of her for having too many famous boyfriends (Jake Gyllenhaal, Calvin Harris, and Harry Styles, among others) and for hanging out with a supermodel girl squad that included Karlie Kloss and Gigi Hadid (who were deemed to be too white, too wealthy, and too thin).

What Swift refers to as "the apocalypse" occurred in 2016. In the song "Famous," which he also produced, Kanye West includes the uninspiring line, "I feel like me and Taylor might still have sex, why, I made that bitch famous." As a result of Swift's outcry, West's ex-wife Kim Kardashian leaked a portion of a taped discussion that seemed to reveal Swift had authorized the lines and called Kardashian a snake. Swift was vindicated in 2020 when the complete conversation was revealed, despite her claims that the bitch phrase had never been stated.

Swift was now a snake at the moment, and #TaylorSwiftIsOverParty was the highest trending subject on Twitter globally.

She vanished for a whole year. She said in Miss Americana that the judgment that she was evil, cunning, and not a nice person was the one from which she truly struggled to recover.

Swift did, however, make a comeback in late 2017 by continuing to write songs that, despite how terrible it may be, reflect her actual life. She performed live with a huge inflatable snake and released the bluntly named album Reputation. I can't even begin to tell you how difficult it was for me not to giggle each time my 63-foot inflatable cobra called Karyn emerged onstage in front of 60,000 adoring fans, she said in a post-tour tweet in 2019. National Snake Day with Taylor Swift.

Since then, she has been more politically loud and outspoken. As a country singer, she was encouraged to stay out of politics, but today she is a supporter of pro-choice abortion rights and an ally of the LGBTQ+ community.

She also came before #MeToo by four years: in 2013, she came out to claim a sexual assault by Denver DJ David Mueller, who had grabbed her behind as she was posing for a picture. After being let off from his work, he sued Swift for $3 million (£1.9 million) in 2015. She then filed a counterclaim for a meager $1. Mueller's defense team said she couldn't have possible seen his hand during the 2017 trial. Because it's in the rear of my body, Swift agreed. Swift triumphed. Again.

Swift's longtime writing partner Liz Rose is most suited to summarize her apparently endless career. The country music website nashnews.com quoted Rose as saying, "She doesn't reinvent herself; she just grows." She is acting just like she always did. She is older and her topics are older. She's merely trying to grow better and progress, and she keeps doing it, unlike many artists who attempt to outwit themselves.

Swift now owns eight homes across the globe, including a $12,000 square foot beach house in Rhode Island and a $20 million (£16 million) penthouse in Manhattan.

However, she prefers to spend the most of her time in Primrose Hill, North London, where she resides with her three cats, Dr. Meredith Grey, Olivia Benson, and Benjamin Button, as well as her actor boyfriend Joe Alwyn, who is from Kent and they have been together for six years. They allegedly met at the 2016 Met Gala in New York, but they didn't begin dating until later that year. This is in contrast to her three-month romance with British actor Tom Hiddleston, which was so widely covered by the media that the two were even accused of staging the relationship for attention. (A charge both disputed.)

She began spending more time in the UK when she started dating Alwyn, and despite having an estimated net worth of $570 million (£468 million), she seems to lead a surprisingly ordinary life (albeit in a townhouse worth £7 million) that is uninteresting to paparazzi. With the exception of the occasional photograph of Swift wearing a hat and scarf, her existence in London is completely overlooked. Her song "London Boy" lists her favorite hangouts, including Camden Market, Brixton, Shoreditch, Hackney, Highgate, and Hampstead Heath (where she watches rugby and meets Alwyn's closest friends at a bar). She sings, "Show me a grey sky, a rainy cab ride..." I adore the English, thank God.

In 'Lavender Haze' on Midnights, she responds to frequent engagement rumors: The only sort of lady they see is a one-night stand or a wife, the song goes. "All they keep asking me is if I'm gonna be your bride."

Swift keeps living a respectable life. Despite their peaceful divorce a decade ago, she has a strong relationship with both of her parents. She continues to be a skilled baker and craftsperson, embroidering baby blankets, plush animals, and other items for her millennial friends who are beginning children. She also revealed her 'dorky' composition techniques this year, categorizing songs into three categories using different fictional pens: Quill Lyrics (for 'antiquated lyrics'), Fountain Pen Lyrics ('contemporary plot'), and Glitter Gel Lyrics ('frivolous, carefree, joyful'). She previously had a genuine quill, but it was broken during an angry moment. Swift is undoubtedly the nerd who inherited the planet, as shown by this level of forensic detail.

It will have been 10 years since that unforgettable pumpkin cake when 2023 approaches. sticky, wet, and somewhat spicy. The genuine stuff, without a doubt.

CHAPTER ELEVEN: Taylor swift Awards

Son Some: 2007: Country Music Association Awards – Horizon Award

2008: American Music Awards – Favorite Female Country Artist (Taylor Swift)

2009: American Music Awards-Favorite Country Album (Fearless)

2010: Capricho Awards-International Singer (Taylor Swift)

2010: Grammy Awards-Album of The Year and Best Country Album (Fearless)

2011: Billboard Music Awards-Top Country Artist (Taylor Swift) 2011: Billboard Music Awards-Top Artist Billboard 200 (Taylor Swift)

2012: Billboard Music Awards-Woman of the Year (Taylor Swift) 2012: American

Music Awards-Favorite Country Album (Speak Now)

2013: MTV Video Music Awards-Best Female Video (I Knew You Were Trouble).

2015: American Music Awards-Favorite Pop / Rock Album (1989) 2015: Brit Awards-International Female Artist (Taylor Swift)

2015: Billboard Music Awards-Top Billboard Album 200 (1989) 2016: Grammy Awards-Best Music Video (Bad Blood)

2016: People's Choice Awards-Favorite Pop Artist (Taylor Swift).

Made in United States
North Haven, CT
08 May 2024

52233785R00095